For

_____

From

_____

_____

Date _____

I am as happy over your
promises as if I had found a
great treasure.

Psalm 119:162

my little
Bible
Promises

Illustrations by
Stephanie McFetridge Britt

Compiled by Brenda C. Ward

A Division of Thomas Nelson Publishers
Since 1798

www.thomasnelson.com

MY LITTLE BIBLE PROMISES
Copyright © 1994 by Tommy Nelson®.
Illustrations © 1994 by Stephanie McFetridge Britt.
All rights reserved. No portion of this book may be
reproduced in any form without written permission of
the publisher, with the exception of brief quotations
in reviews.
Published in Nashville, Tennessee, by Tommy
Nelson®, a Division of Thomas Nelson, Inc. Visit us
on the web at www.tommynelson.com.
Scripture quotations are from the *International
Children's Bible®, New Century Version®*, copyright ©
1986, 1988, 1999 by Tommy Nelson®, a Division of
Thomas Nelson, Inc.
Scripture entries marked KJV are from the *King James
Version*.
Tommy Nelson® books may be purchased in bulk for
educational, business, fundraising, or sales promotion-
al use. For information, please email
SpecialMarkets@ThomasNelson.com.

ISBN: 0-8499-1145-1
ISBN: 1-4003-0649-3 (2005 edition)
Printed in China
05 06 07 08 09 LEO 9 8 7 6 5 4 3 2 1

Contents

GOD
WILL BE
WITH
YOU

You can be sure that I will be with you always. I will continue with you until the end of the world.

Matthew 28:20

Come near to God, and
God will come near to you.

James 4:8

You will search for me.
And when you search for me
with all your heart, you will
find me!

Jeremiah 29:13

16

Being with you will fill me with joy. At your right hand I will find pleasure forever.

Psalm 16:11

I will live with them and walk with them. And I will be their God. And they will be my people.

2 Corinthians 6:16

Those who know the Lord
trust him. He will not leave
those who come to him.

Psalm 9:10

GOD WILL GUIDE YOU

The Lord says, "I will make you wise. I will show you where to go. I will guide you and watch over you."

Psalm 32:8

Lord, you give light to my lamp. The Lord brightens the darkness around me.

2 Samuel 22:29

The Lord himself will go
before you. He will be with
you. He will not leave you or
forget you.

Deuteronomy 31:8

This God is our God forever and ever. He will guide us from now on.

Psalm 48:14

You keep your loving promise. You lead the people you have saved.

Exodus 15:13

But the Spirit gives love,
joy, peace, patience, kindness,
goodness, faithfulness,
gentleness, self-control. . . .
We get our new life from the
Spirit. So we should follow
the Spirit.

Galatians 5:22-25

God Will Take Care Of You

Give your worries to the Lord. He will take care of you.

Psalm 55:22

So our hope is in the Lord. He is our help, our shield to protect us.

Psalm 33:20

You are my hiding place.
You protect me from my
troubles. You fill me with
songs of salvation.

Psalm 32:7

Look at the birds in the air.
They don't plant or harvest or
store food in barns. But your
heavenly Father feeds the
birds. And you know that you
are worth much more than
the birds.

Matthew 6:26

GOD
WILL
BLESS
YOU

Blessed are the pure in heart: for they shall see God.

Matthew 5:8 (KJV)

You give me a better way to
live. So I live as you want
me to.

2 Samuel 22:37

Every good action and every perfect gift is from God.

James 1:17

Blessed are the peacemakers:
for they shall be called the
children of God.

Matthew 5:9 (KJV)

Those who love your
teachings will find true peace.
Nothing will defeat them.

Psalm 119:165

GOD WILL FORGIVE YOU

Yes, if you forgive others for the things they do wrong, then your Father in heaven will also forgive you for the things you do wrong.

Matthew 6:14

Lord, if you punished people for all their sins, no one would be left. But you forgive us. So you are respected.

Psalm 130:3-4

Everyone who believes in
Jesus will be forgiven. God
will forgive his sins through
Jesus.

Acts 10:43

Do not be angry with each other, but forgive each other. If someone does wrong to you, then forgive him. Forgive each other because the Lord forgave you.

Colossians 3:13

We can trust God. He does what is right. He will make us clean from all the wrongs we have done.

I John 1:9

God
Will
Answer
You

Continue to ask, and God will give to you. Continue to search, and you will find. Continue to knock, and the door will open for you.

Matthew 7:7

The Lord sees the good people. He listens to their prayers.

Psalm 34:15

God listens to us every time we ask him. So we know that he gives us the things that we ask from him.

I John 5:15

Wait for the Lord's help. Be strong and brave and wait for the Lord's help.

Psalm 27:14

He will answer the prayers
of the needy. He will not
reject their prayers.

Psalm 102:17

GOD WILL ALWAYS LOVE YOU

Christ's love is greater than any person can ever know. But I pray that you will be able to know that love. Then you can be filled with the fullness of God.

Ephesians 3:19

The Father has loved us so much! He loved us so much that we are called children of God.

I John 3:1

So these three things
continue forever: faith, hope
and love. And the greatest of
these is love.

I Corinthians 13:13

Give thanks to the Lord
because he is good. His love
continues forever.

Psalm 136:1

Stephanie McFetridge Britt is a freelance illustrator for books, greeting cards, and magazines. She has illustrated over 30 children's books. Prior to her freelance work, Britt worked six years for Hallmark Cards, Inc. She and her husband live in Hawaii.